THE BUDDHA in ME

Written by
Christine H. Huynh, M.D.

Illustrated by
Mariia Luzina

Dharma Wisdom, LLC

The Buddha in Me
Bringing the Buddha's Teachings into Practice series
Copyright © 2021 by Dharma Wisdom, LLC

Dharma Wisdom, LLC
Arlington, Texas
www.DharmaWisdomDW.com
books@DharmaWisdomDW.com

Author: Christine H. Huynh, M.D.
Illustrator: Mariia Luzina
Designer: Lucia Benito

Library of Congress
Control Number:
2020925122

ISBN: 978-1-951175-07-8

First Edition 2021

The Buddha was a prince who lived long ago around 624-544 B.C.E. His name was Siddhartha Gautama. He was a human being, just like me. "Siddhartha" means one who is accomplished and has lived a meaningful life.

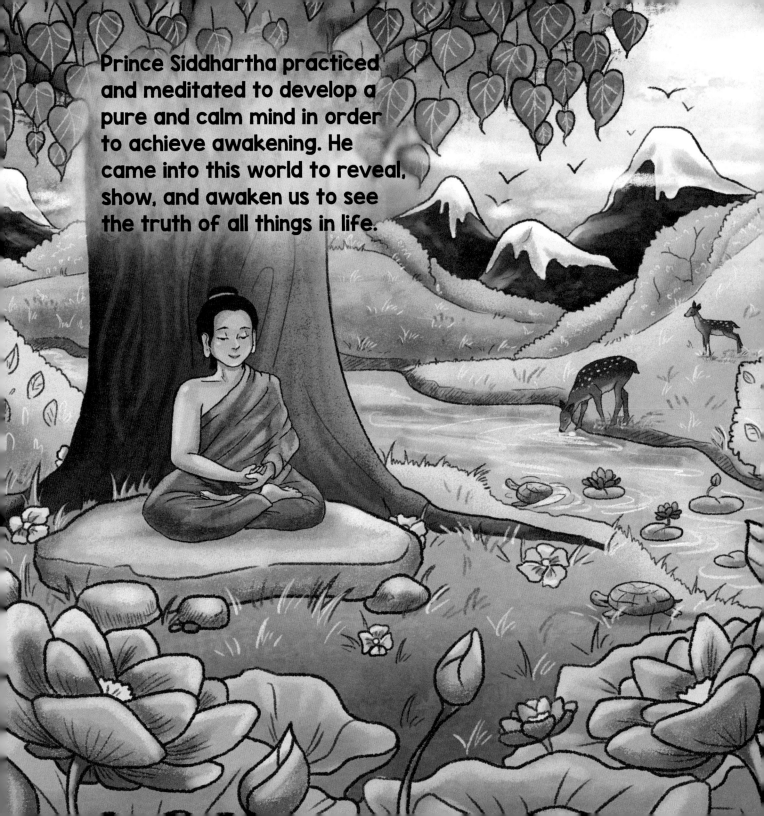

Prince Siddhartha practiced and meditated to develop a pure and calm mind in order to achieve awakening. He came into this world to reveal, show, and awaken us to see the truth of all things in life.

He is called the Buddha because he has this wonderful Awakening. The word "Buddha" comes from the Sanskrit word "Bodhi," which means full awakening and understanding the true nature of things. He is the Shakyamuni Buddha. Shakya is the name of his family's clan in India, and Muni means living with compassion, patience, harmony, and purity.

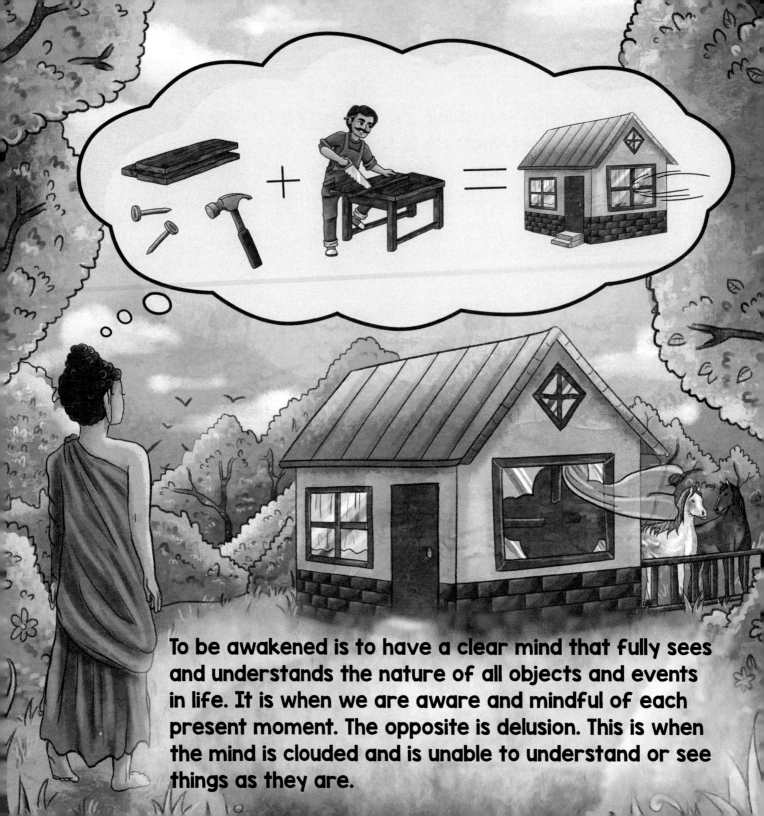

To be awakened is to have a clear mind that fully sees and understands the nature of all objects and events in life. It is when we are aware and mindful of each present moment. The opposite is delusion. This is when the mind is clouded and is unable to understand or see things as they are.

The Buddha has the wisdom from deep reflection and is aware of every thought, speech, and action. He is compassionate toward all living beings whether they are from live births (like me), egg-laying animals (like the swan), birth in the soil (like the worms), or birth through changes in forms (like cocoons changing to butterflies).

He teaches that everyone has this Buddha-nature – a true mind that is always clear and bright. I must learn more about the Buddha so that I can practice his virtues and allow my Buddha-nature to shine and be the best I can be.

The Buddha is the World-Honored One with ten great qualities.

He is considered a Jewel because it is rare for us to find a great being like him.

I) The Buddha is called the Tathagata /Tata-gata/, the one who has a solid mind and is not shaken by the changes in life. He teaches me how to comfort myself when I am sad, like when my dog is hurt or when my toy breaks.

I learn to accept that things change in life. I can see the mother dog in her puppy. Old things get recycled and become parts of new things again, so nothing is lost! I recycle my broken toy so its parts can be used for new toys.

2) The Buddha deserves to receive gift offerings because I respect him as my teacher. He shows me the Way to live and is the teacher of all teachers. He is the king of all objects and events because he understands them and has the answers to put an end to every problem.

I can earn respect from my friends by showing them the Dharma path. I can teach them how to practice for their Buddha-nature to awaken and shine. First is to learn from listening and reading. Second, think and reflect on what is learned. Third, act with mindfulness to have right thoughts, speech, and actions.

3) The Buddha has a deep and complete understanding of all things in the world.

He attained this by reflecting inward to understand himself and others. He is able to see the true nature of everything. He can see that the flower is not really a flower by itself, as it is made up of non-flower elements such as sunshine, rain water, and soil nutrients combined.

I practice looking inward so I can understand myself and others. I understand why my friend got upset when I ate the last cookie. I would feel mad too if my friend did not share the last cookie with me.

From reflecting, I am able to see my true nature. I have my grandfather's eyes and smile. He is always with me even though he is not here anymore.

4) The Buddha has perfect wisdom and action. He applies his deep thoughts to carry out his actions skillfully. He has great compassion that brings happiness and relieves sorrow for others.

I practice being aware of my thoughts and feelings. This way, I will think before I speak and act so that each of my words and actions do not make my parents or friends feel sad. First, I need to realize my feelings. Then, I think about whether this feeling is good or bad and determine how I should react.

Lastly, I will speak and act in a way that will bring happiness to everyone. This is how I practice the Muni character of compassion.

5) The Buddha is able to overcome all difficulties. He knows who to talk to and what to do in any situation. He knows when, where, and how to solve problems. He calms and makes everyone feel comfortable in any troubling conditions.

I can practice the same way. When I am angry, I wait to cool down before I speak to my friend who upset me. I should do it in our private treehouse and speak with loving-kindness. This way, I do not say or do things that I will regret when my mind is agitated. This is how I practice the Muni character of patience.

6) The Buddha provides the path to solve the problems of the world. He tells me to develop right thoughts, speech, and actions, instead of wrong thoughts, speech, and actions.

7) The Buddha is the greatest practitioner. He practices to the endpoint until he achieves the complete awakening and awareness. He has great diligence and does not let distractions interfere with his practice.

I must practice and practice and never give up so I can have a calm and clear mind. It will then help me achieve awakening by being aware of my thoughts, speech, and actions. This mindfulness will help me be the best person I can be for my family and friends.

8) The Buddha manages his mind and influences everyone to follow the right path. He is a hero with great strength who can ease the negative seeds, such as sadness and anger. Instead, he waters the positive seeds of happiness and loving-kindness. He sets the perfect example for me to learn and follow.

I can practice to be a good role model for my sister. When I have feelings of jealousy, I practice so that my mind develops thoughts of love and giving. When my younger sister beat me in a game of chess, I congratulated her with a hug.

Congratulations!

My mother was happy and rewarded us with an ice cream sundae. This is how I practice the Muni character of harmony.

I pray that my practice will help the birds in the sky, my friends on Earth, and the worms in the ground.

10) The Buddha is the fully Awakened One. He attained this awakening all by himself. He has the complete and perfect awakening. He is kind to show this awakening to me and everyone else.

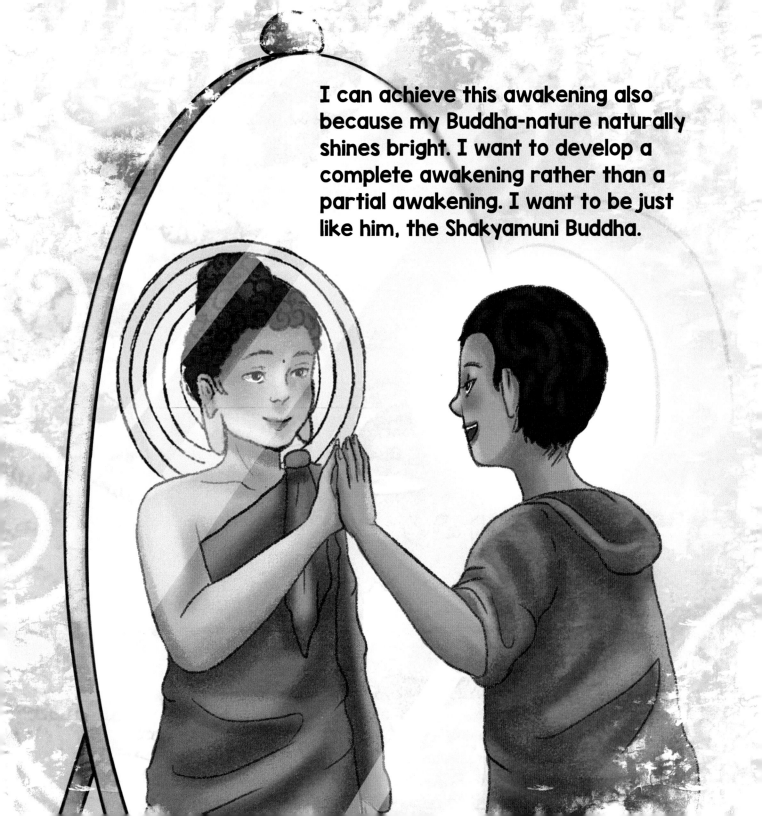

I can achieve this awakening also because my Buddha-nature naturally shines bright. I want to develop a complete awakening rather than a partial awakening. I want to be just like him, the Shakyamuni Buddha.

I must first calm my mind and look deeply within myself. I do this by following my breath as it flows in and out. Then, I can see much clearer to understand myself, others, and all situations. This allows me to be aware of what my mind is thinking in each present moment. This is how I practice the Muni character of purity.

I can be aware of all my thoughts. I can be aware of the nature of things that I see and hear. I can be aware of what I want to say and what I do say. I can be aware of all my actions. When I am mindful, I will think of good thoughts, speak with loving-kindness, and perform actions that benefit others as well as myself.

From learning the ten merits of the Buddha, I can remember to develop these good qualities and apply them to my daily life. I do not have to look very far to find the Buddha, as the Buddha-nature is already inside of me.

I must practice to keep it clear and bright so I can bring out my Muni characters of compassion, patience, harmony, and purity.